Muneera Pilgrim is an  er,
writer, broadcaster and T

She conducts worksh s
alternative ways to tell stc
ideas.

She regularly contributes to BBC Radio 2's *Pause for Thought*. She is a community artist-researcher, a mental health professional, and an alumni associate artist with the English Touring Theatre, where she is working on her first play.

Muneera has written for the Guardian, Amaliah, Huffington Post, the Independent, Al Jazeera, Black Ballad, and various other digital and print platforms. She has been featured across the BBC network, as well as Sky News, Sky Arts and Al Jazeera. In 2015 a documentary about her former group Poetic Pilgrimage was commissioned by Al Jazeera. *Hip-Hop Hijabis* has been screened several times since.

Muneera holds an MA in Islamic studies, where she focused on Black British pathways to spirituality, migration, gender and race, and she holds a second MA in Women's Studies, where she focused on the intersection of faith and spirituality, race, gender, autoethnography and methodologies of empowerment for non-centred people. Her innovation in her work won her the Ann Kaloski-Naylor Award for Adventurous Academic Writing.

C000301079

That Day She'll Proclaim Her Chronicles

Muneera Pilgrim

Burning Eye

BurningEyeBooks
Never Knowingly
Mainstream

Copyright © 2021 Muneera Pilgrim

The author asserts the moral right under the Copyright, Designs and Patents Act 1988 to be identified as the author of this work.

All rights reserved. No part of this publication may be reproduced, stored in a retrieval system, or transmitted, in any form or by any means without the prior written consent of the author, nor be otherwise circulated in any form of binding or cover other than that in which it is published and without a similar condition being imposed on the subsequent purchaser.

This edition published by Burning Eye Books 2021

www.burningeye.co.uk

@burningeyebooks

Burning Eye Books
15 West Hill, Portishead, BS20 6LG

ISBN 978-1-913958-06-0

THAT
DAY
SHE'LL
PROCLAIM
HER
CHRONICLES

To the memory of my late godmother, Eileen Mignott.
Thank you for being an example of a joyful Black woman.

بِسْمِ اللَّهِ الرَّحْمَنِ الرَّحِيْمِ

When the earth is shaken with its quake,
and the earth brings out its load,
and man (bewildered and baffled) will say, *What has
happened to her?*
that day she'll proclaim her chronicles,
for her Lord will have inspired it.

Quran Surah 99:1–5

CONTENTS

WAXING

OPENING

An evening in the summer of 1980.
The night is shy.
Clouds brim red
so full they swell and blast the sky
bright blush, deep rouge,
the kinds of red dark-skinned girls grew up thinking were not
    for them.
The day cannot say goodbye.
Birds are humming a sunset song;
the sky refuses to listen.
Summer solstice a few days away,
198 days until the year's end.

Skin still sore,
skull still busted,
sons are still grounded.
Police prowl to exert control.
Bristol has not recovered from St Pauls.

My mother is in the kitchen boiling a brew.
I am restless,
riotous stirring
in her belly.
This is the calm before the storm.

SWEETBACK

I open the twelve-inch cardboard envelope
the colour of dirty sand,
pull out the white paper sleeve
made to hug the black vinyl,
walk, disc balancing between my upright palms.

It hits the deck and spins,
33 rpm,
pin grips suspended
on the edge of this whirling black orb,
no beginning nor end,
slightly warped, and spinning.

I back away from the player,
sink into the soft edges of my bed.
The first note holds like it is gasping for breath.
I am the centre of the story.

I don't know about African American matriarchs
cooking grits or collard greens.
I've never witnessed my grandma sitting
on a veranda singing
God hymns while puffing a pipe,
though I know she did.

I'm more second generation,
Jamaican in Britain:
Gran's house and Saturday soup,
blue or white vans picking me up for Sunday school.

Every other cousin was a soundman
with a stack system in their room.

I was more knock out ginger but home before eight,
defrost the chicken, Mum's coming back late.
But the words speak to me.
You will rise.

I feel the blood in my body stirring.
A long list of nameless women
unfurls inside the coat of my skin.

Prayers do travel through vinyl;
a song is a sanctuary filled
with *Our Fathers, Amens and Ameens*.
Notes can be mutiny, Morant Bay rebellion,
lyrics our litany,
          our modern-day psalms.

BLUE MAGIC

All that you touch
You Change.
All that you Change
Changes you.
The only lasting truth
Is Change.
God is Change.

Octavia E Butler, *Parable of the Sower*

Arched into submission
like the Prophet who split
the moon;
holy books missed her
as she parts midway.
She grabs the root, forages to the scalp,
threads her fingers through the forest
and untangles spirals wound.
Doughy, warm, grease.
The colour of Turkish motifs
sits on the back of her carob-tone palm.
She is like a scaffold;
her legs house the body sat between them,
the final element to her blue magic.
Box Braids, Flat Twist, Two Strands,
the story of how comb became instrument
to construct crowns.

SKIN A CAT

*Wah gwan ah ere, nah gwan ah hell, 'cause the devil will not
allow it.*

My dad

My mum talks about death like family
members coming to visit;
she wants the carpets cleaned and the walls
in the corridor painted before they arrive.
My father lets *if Gad speer mi life* stalk sentences like a shadow,
or the dot beneath the *bah.*

On the top of my mother's coconut-flesh-coloured wardrobe,
over the compartment with her church and wedding hats with
     the lace trim
that looks like cobwebs the way that dust clings,
pushed right to the back is my mother's hospital grip.

If you were to pull it down,
dust it off, fiddle with the rusting latches,
the top would flip back and you would see
silk pyjamas, night dresses, full slips and petticoats,
a washbag with an unused flannel and a pair of pink slippers
     with a bow;
look at how prepared
for death we are, how close to dying we are.

As a kid before I left the house, I was told to cream my legs
and make sure my pants were clean
in case I had to be rushed to hospital.
Years later I realised the world sees us as dirty,
and maybe my mother thought some
Vaseline, Pond's or Palmer's shimmering on my legs
would buy us shreds of dignity.
Make the person handling my limp body think,
She is a child worth saving, a child that is loved.

Sister Fiasah said she'd always dress her little girls with gold;
it said to the world they come from a home.
Our parents were always thinking of subtle ways to preserve
    our life
yet in the same breath preparing to die.

I brought you into this world, and I will take you out
was used to scare us kids into submission.
*Rather you fear me than go outside and risk making mistakes that
    end your life,*
like wrong place at the wrong time, right place at the wrong time,
being Black in your skin.

We are preparing to die,
and I've known this since the day I was born.

But to be murdered took me longer to understand,
murdered like Yvonne Ruddock, Sarah Reed, Shukri Abdi,
different means, same death.

BLACK CHERRY LIPSTICK

Now, we too have the ability
to be desirable, a gang
to which dark-skinned girls
can belong.

Inked our lips for you,
you stick of magic
adorning our faces
like bronze.

You always knew how to seduce us,
back corners of shops
where assistants knew
not to assist.

LESSONS TAUGHT TO GIRLS AND BOYS

1.
We have been taught
to endure rape,
to ignore rape,
to accept rape,
to be raped,
to love rape,
that it's not rape,

and many of us obey like the good little girls we are.
Then we get older, realise we are planets populous,
filled to the brim with victims and survivors
living under our skin,
some of whom were too young to consent;
others eventually said yes, because he dismissed no(s).

So what is there to do but sit in circles
or on group chats comparing notes,
the many ways we were forced
even though we didn't know?
I'm not saying it was rape, but…
has become a coming-of-age slogan

I'm not saying it was rape,
but… I was fourteen and he was twenty-seven.
I'm not saying it was rape,
but… he shouted when I tried to go.
I'm not saying it was rape,
but… I thought I owed him or something.
I'm not saying it was rape.
Surely we can't all have been raped.

2.

Others learnt the roles they should play from stories,
nursery rhymes and kiss chase.
Run, fast, faster, as fast you can, don't stop, drop or lose your breath,
for they are beasts parading as men,
boys being moulded into beasts.
A few years later the same boys will pull at bra straps;
you will be accused of flirting with them.
The boys will witness you
walking home from school in all your fourteen-year-old glory,
baby hairs stuck down with Jam!,
school tie loosened around neck,
grey pleated skirt bunched under your white shirt.
There is nothing grown about you,
only where some desire to place you.
Grown men with wives will drive by in flashy cars in hopes of
f**king you senseless.

RECOLLECTION

At the point that his hand pushes your head
so hard you hear the click of your neck,
the dull rattle of your brain,
your legs are in shock and you have fallen to your knees,
It is then you will realise he is not here to just kiss.

So fast it must be a skill, or at least well rehearsed.
It is normally an abandoned place,
or a place where no one knows
your name and everyone knows his.
You try to remember the route home;
your body will not have processed
what is going to happen next,
but you will know that you need to remember
the way home.

He will growl somethings at you,
maybe even slap you in the face.
As he unzips his jeans,
you will sit there and think about school,
lessons, friends, teachers, anything but this.
Juggle these thoughts in your mind for a while.

Once you've made it home
it will replay over
and over again,
but then it will fade.

Years later you will be brunching with friends
like intruders who enter gated mansions with rose gardens,
water sprinklers and high walls.
The memory will come back for you, drag you under,
leave you gasping for breath.
Once again you will be frozen,
trying to remember your route home.

CANEROW

I don't know how to canerow.
My mother never taught me,
her mother never taught her,
her mother bought her
clothes, shipped them in broad barrels
with brown bodies and silver rims
across the Atlantic,
a synonym for love.

Over the fossil of Black bones
and brave hearts,
those who became mami wata
centuries before.
Them, in ruku or sujood
on the bed of the sea.
Ships coursing over them once again,
this time in the cargo hold: barrels, not bodies.

My mother never taught me how to sew
or how to marinate curry goat.
She never said,
If you are lucky men will steal your heart
while others will grab at body parts
and pick away at your safety like fruit.

There are a few things I did not tell her too.
I never told her about the boys I slept with,
the money I owe.
The days I contemplated ending it all,
the fights I had,
the times I made stupid decisions
and could have
lost my life, but I jumped in the car anyway.
I am sure she's kept those days
secret from me too.
Silence is also a synonym for love.

COUSINS

A three-seater sofa with seven bodies
who have at least one facial feature just like mine:
lips, eyes or nose.

Grazed legs, bubblegum-breathed bodies,
siblings from my mother's mother's womb.
With them I sit learning lessons on living.

Like the one whose bras I inherited
because overnight, I went from
flat-chested to emerging mounds.

When we could not afford a bag of chips,
the one who propositioned Mr Ling
and got us a portion of crispies for just 25p.

The one who taught me the art of protesting
to save the petrol station where we got our stash
of wine gums from.

The one who taught me jam
wasn't just for toast; it also tasted great
with fried egg and escovitch fish.

The one who I roamed with
for hours after school; a beating
was a risk we were willing to take.

This is a special dedication
for the naughty ones who
caused the trouble but never got the blame.

The one who lassoed
cats above their head
to demonstrate the speed of light.

The ones I sang songs with like 'Gimme Punani',
but we were too scared to ask what *punani* is,
because the last time we asked about a song
with strange words, we got chopped in our heads.

This is especially for those
who played knock out ginger
in the thick molasses of night,

sneaking through back doors
of house parties and dead yards,
dribbling onto the streets like ghosts.

From the ones who
cried when they got cussed to the ones
who muttered under their breaths, 'Fixup.'

This is for my summer holiday cousins
who lived in different cities
and it would take us a day or two to reacquaint.

The calypso queens
and carnival hot girls,
DJs and soundmen,
Pathfinder leaders,
the ones who've now gone,
to my cousins who were old since the day I was born.

This is for the cousins who came from different countries,
slept in our rooms, showed us
the meaning of hard work,

sending money back home, teaching me it is not
only in the hearts of people with my facial features,
but there are also places that I might belong.

THAWED

The joke is on us,
baked beans on chips with a blob of tomato ketchup generation,
go get the belt generation.
Call Childline and I will beat them too.
White vans pick us up for Sunday School.
Pick the oxtail out of the Saturday soup
and the kidney beans out of the red pea stew.
Finger aerials from MIDI systems;
gotta get rid of the static so you can listen
to DJ Styles on your FM dial.
But first,
defrost the chicken
before Mum gets home.

As you rummage through the freezer
your hand strikes gold,
but by now you should know
the joke is on us.
Plastic containers are never filled
with ice cream,
always rice and peas or mutton from last week:
our culture packed in plastic containers, with pictures of fake flavours,
deep frozen for later consumption.
It's never the same once it has thawed.
If England is an ice box,
my generation is not the same as the first,
though we have thawed.

SOUND SYSTEM SPEAKER BOXES

Punches the air,
permeates the atmosphere.
Shakes the ground beneath us.
Black boxes with round holes
stacked higher than odds,
kissing the sky,
grounded by mics and hefty cables
rooted into the spine.
Through the blast waves
the bass mumbles and blows a low tone,
subtle aroma of our tales embalmed in sound.
Our prayers embroidered,
weaved and cross-stitched into the
seams of our soul,
pressed onto vinyl.
Rotating black orb causes storms,
ruptures the divides of time.
What looks like a sound system speaker box
and people leaned
up or dancing
is a TARDIS or slang
for Black folk communing with their past and future
kin.

MIS-SOLD

They left before blankets of milk
made rivers from streets
and mosquitoes and dust
curdled in its cream.

They left before shooting made hell of Hope Road,
and the green gold that used to grow was no longer enough
to sustain farmers and their homes.

Left before corrugated rooftops flapped around
like the wings of birds,
churches ripped from their roots,
flipped on their side when caught in Gilbert's eye.

Left before the IMF came in with aid solutions
and traded education and dignity for billboards of
bucket deals, biscuits and mouthwatering KFC.

They were lucky,
This is what they tell me.
But what if my grandad said he was sorry,
my grandma said she would stay,
never left the land, never came to England, never sought warmth
in a paraffin heater in a room that refused to heat on City Road?

What if she never cleaned, choired and nursed
elderly people younger than her?
What would our life look like then?

19 WOODBOROUGH STREET

*Your name is upon my tongue your image is in my sight
your memory is in my heart where can I send these words
that I write?*

Rumi

I see myself skipping through the hallway
in sepia tone or monochrome,
a little girl holding your widemouthed white metal mug
with the blue rim.
When I grow up I want a Jamaican plate set like yours.

You hum Jesus songs;
your choir is nothing without you.
You grate ginger,
the juiced-up shreds left to the side
so *it gets likkle air* before you place it in the rice pot
brimming with water, hellfire hot.
Always a Dutch pot on top of the stove,
Birmingham harddough bread next to the fridge
for dipping into stew,
for devouring,
drops of brown stew chicken all over my clothes and fingertips.
You call my name.
I've been quiet for far too long.
I thought remembering would be proof enough.

WHEN GOD ENTERS A ROOM

Your brother runs upstairs to play
Sonic on his Mega Drive.
You realise you have forgotten
your glass of dilute squash.
It's coming up to two,
and old church people's timing is impeccable.
You skitter through the kitchen,
sliding around on your white socks,
gliding back and forth like you are the king of pop.

As you are about to race upstairs,
someone calls your name.
Sister Telford has seen you; you cannot escape.
You lead her to the living room.
Your mother says you must stay.
God is not here yet,
or she's waiting to let it be known.

They arrive one by one
like the counsel of a secret society,
or mafiosi at lunch.
They proceed with hymns from the brown book
with the gold cross and the crisp pages.
They read scriptures, calm,
like they don't know what is next.
You stare at the man in the checked suit.
He takes out his kerchief and says, 'Now let's pray.'
They stand up, hands in the air, eyes closed;
even the lady with the walking stick is momentarily healed.
You can't close your eyes;
no matter how many times you have seen it, there is something
about them balling drops of sweat from their foreheads,
the words they speak in some ancient tongue,
something about their raised voices,
about their stamping feet,
about their demands to God to reveal herself;
they are blown blossom in a cyclone lost in their own sway.

THREE WOMEN

I'm not made of the stuff of my parents,
nor the family who received them
when England became their home.
When my mum arrived
she thought the houses were factories.
She tells me of work, duties, and stinking bed pails.
She tells me of cleaning bodies limber and lifeless
as breath departs,
of matron who doesn't like the colour of her skin,
houses with no heating,
how she started losing her hearing
and how deep the snow would fall.

I'm her wash belly pickney and one girlchild.
I cried all the time, she tells me,
and I believe it, because I still do,
a body of fever trying to cool itself down.
I do in the dark and into pillows so no one can hear
I cry because I am
a bag of guilt and
mixed emotions,
a helping of anxiety
and constant fear.
I am expectations I can't live up to.
Don't know if I'll be able to do things like my mum.

Sista Mama,
burly, stoic, jovial and kind.
I don't know when she came to the country,
but watching these women I learn about responsibility.
My mother cares for Sista Mama like she is her new baby,
Sista Mama's tears more noble than mine.
A memory like a fading fog
but clear enough to identify pain.
She just about makes out faces,
on good days recalls a handful of names.

She cries; she doesn't want me and my mum to go.
We tell her it's the COVID and that's why we can't stay.
But she is in too much pain,
broken heart,
broken body,
broken mind.
I can see she doesn't believe us.
She does not know where she is,
let alone of COVID;
all she knows is she did her duty,
worked hard to serve this family,
and now we are making excuses for why we must go.

THE WOMEN OF MY FAMILY: THROWBACK SUITE 1

> *Melanin rich and honeyed, butter brown syrupy*
> *Da blacker the berry, the sweeter the sweet*
> *Girl, all hues of the ebony rainbow shine*
> *Our rind so rare, age like fine wine*
> *Lips plump like cherries ready to be picked*
> *Dey spend all kind of money tryin' to look like dis*
> DB Mays, *Black Lives, Lines, & Lyrics*

The women of my family are graceful, insightful, wise, sensitive,
independent, interdependent and dependable,
depending on what's called for at any given time.
Giving and supportive women,
their words more soothing than the smoothest of soothsayers.
Maroon cushioned lips, rounded hips and backs
so straight they lead up to heaven's gate.

Mary Magdalene meets Nana the Maroon,
the Blue and White Nile eloping in the centre of Khartoum,
Joan of Arc, Sojourner Truth, Rabia al-Adawiyya, Zulaika,
Makidah, Frida Kahlo, Nikki Giovanni, Phoolan Devi,
Haggar min as Sudan, wife of a prophet and mother of a nation.

The women of my family contain them all.
They are so gifted it's almost mythic;
at minimum they are mystic.

I wouldn't have believed it if I didn't see it with my own eyes,
breathe it in like the kiss of life,
the horizons after the night skies.

They are the thread of white that separates day from night,
the specks of black fading from my grandmother's eyes.
This seems to be the hukm of becoming wise,

the hukm of leading a rich life and
giving abundantly like a willow tree
with an endless amount of leaves.
Not even autumn can shake you,
like a stake firmly rooted in the earth,
balancing the planet and all of God's creation.
I've bore witness to women who make something out of
nothing,
sense out of nonsense.
I would tell you I've seen them battle demons,
but you would swear that it's a lie,
but what is the beating of drums
at a kumina under Jamaican moonlit skies?

What is women lined up in church sanctuaries,
speaking with the authority of God?
Healing the sick with their prayers,
feeding the poor with their prayers,
because they know
the streets of England are not paved with gold.
The stories they were told that made them leave their homes
were baseless, but these women are the gold that pave the
streets.
I've sat in circles with women drenched in something
between sweat and tears, women of all years,
calling her name until thy kingdom come,
thy will be done, here and now,
we desire healing and you are the one who we believe in.
And though we may call the divine by a different name,
them showing me, she is only one
and that one has blessed me with my mum.
So God bless the women who've raised me;
 indeed they are gracious and gold!

WANING

CAMINO

People flock to London like pilgrims
hoping the ground beneath them will seep into their flesh,

wrench open their core,
navigate through the body like blood.

I left Bristol in search of enlightenment,
to breathe without negotiating breath.

Thought I could find it in clothes, or hiding
in the faces of Black folk
on the tube at Grove after Portobello.

I found scraps of my reflection painted
on walls and dance floors,
scooped them up like a miner who'd just found gold.

LIKE

The first time you donned box braids
or got your head shaved.
The first time you sipped rosé.
Emancipation.
Naming your country for the first time.
Elected prime minister
before we knew it would end like this.
Having enough food to feed your kids.
The gap-toothed smile on your son's face
as he grapples sweetcorn or chicken wings.
Paper travel cards with the date rubbed out
and the day ahead.
Black Cherry lipstick.
Black Lycra miniskirts.
Black leggings with the lace bottoms in the late nineties.
Black girls discovering there is more to lipstick
than *Black Cherry* by Revlon.
Belly out.
Bra off.
Chin up.
Boots on.
Divorce.
Honey-coated divorce.
There are countless ways to experience free.

FREEDOM

Underwhelmed was my first impression.
Pine floorboards with matching tables.
Bar staff with black T-shirts, matching aprons,
smiley faces, but a cliché at best.
Orchestrated, like
everyone had the same modelling agent.
I was not convinced.
With the expectation of rapture still in her eyes
Dionne said, 'Are you ready to go in?'
I realised then this was not the final destination.
Black folk huddled at the door
on the other side of the room
should have been a clue.
We walked across the floor.
Muffled music padded the air.
Red lights echoed and adorned our faces,
bouncing off us, the mirror and the stairs.
I wish I had not trivialised that moment we cascaded,
paid more attention to our glide toward the door.
Pushing it open was like breaking water and light beaming in.
There were no bodies holding up the walls.
No *screw face* hiding fears or inhibitions.
No tensions needing to be defused.
No fear of fights
or having to leave early to avoid a madness.
Songs I had never heard but felt like they'd lulled me when I
    was young.
I outstretched my arms.
Time seeped into all the dancing bodies,
including my own.
Movement slowed down,
soft shadows and silhouettes swaying to the DJ's spin.
We looked like a living photo,
the type you'd find in a museum in years to come.

Circa 2003: Arms in the Air
Blown bodies
Dancing like sand in a storm
An illustration of what it might look like to feel free

RED LIPSTICK

*As Black women, there is not enough of us not to be an
ally to each other.*

Mena Fombo

On one hand makeup
on the other a tool
emblem of sisterhood

arms, struggle, home.
We fought our way
earned the right

to pop colour on our cushioned lips.
Beautify the world with our gift
signs that we are here on the collar of white shirts.

Pose for the 'gram, pout with our friends
tell ourselves we are beautiful
and with our body make amends.

LUMINOUS

*O Allah, place light in my heart, and on my tongue light, and
in my ears light and in my sight light, and above me light, and
below me light, and to my right light, and to my left light, and
before me light and behind me light. Place in my soul light.
Magnify for me light, and amplify for me light…*

Dua of Light

Half two, and the barbershops are brimming
        on Stapleton Road, a mother negotiating
           her son's first trim.
There are queues of cars outside the Senegalese
        car wash, tasbihs hanging from each rear-view mirror.
          A boy, no more than seventeen,

bends to tie the laces of his girlfriend's Air Force 1s
        while she continues speaking into her phone.
           The man in Beauty Queen puts *two for the price
of one* on bundles of X-Pressions 27-inch purple hair.
        Rotisserie chicken spins outside the Lebanese café;
          two uncles stand in the doorway of
the Three Black Birds disputing whether pimento
        or thyme is best to flavour mackerel rundown,
          all before agreeing the breadfruit from
across the road is *wata belly* and overpriced.
        Fearless of spillage from syrup mixed with
          crushed ice, the sky juice man looks ready

for an all-white rave. The church sisters are on the side
        of the boy at the bus stop, such that when police
          try to stop and search,
the sisters rebuke them in the name of Christ the Lord,
        and it seems Jesus hears, because they relent.
          The Roadman helps the old woman across

the street with her shopping; they speak about the
        rising price of food, and how in her day there
                were more helpful young men like him.
He feels good for the first time in a long time.
        Mercedes and Maserati are driving with their tops
                down, or windows open. A crew of cyclists

fly by with Skepta and Wizkid playing through their
        speakers. Days like this when the air is scarce
                and the sun beats down to compete with
the light of the everyday people who decorate the streets,
        they are lighthouses, or lanterns at least.

ST PAUL'S FESTIVAL

i

The string section of Starvue's 'Body Fusion' fills the air
　　like a collapsing canopy of summer rain.
I suspect the speakers stacked off Thomas Street
　　are Toyboy VIP. We wade

into the centre of the constellations, where everyone
　　wants to dance, scared to be the first.
Bellies drunk from the sun's heat, a residue of glow
　　sits on our skin. We twirl, hold hands,

circle each other the way heavenly bodies and girls
　　on a dance floor do. A paving slab dance floor,
sacred circle of women's handbags and summer jackets,
　　our wings extended, eyes closed, spinning,

we become mother figures for white girls from Clifton
　　scared of this part of town on any other day,
and I would be offended by them asking
　　if I sold weed on any other day, but today

is different.

ii

Dressed like extras from a Puma Jamaica campaign,
　　we roam streets like a pack of gazelles
lost in the lines of Arabic love poetry.

Night falls. Beenie Man blares from Campbell Street.
　　On a garden wall, we hold polystyrene boxes the colour
of stars, filled with jerk and festival, one-handed,

trying to locate Orion's belt with the other.

iii

They stalk Black boys.
        Unaware, those boys

compare trainers,
    mock a friend too scared
to speak   to a girl.
Vipers with truncheons and badges
    see warm-blooded Black boys as food.

Everything goes
    blank,   more void
than black holes.

I find myself   spitting bars
    in faces   about this

being our ends.   Babylon
    must burn,   and we fought
for these streets,

Yashima so fired
    she becomes   comet

and blue flame.

iv

Coconut from the gizzada stuck in our teeth,
we journey home, to lie on a single bed

pretending we will not fall asleep.
Still looking at stars.

RAGGA FM

Black orb.
Obsidian disco ball.
Midnight malachite.
Black planet with a hole in its core.
Black hole drawing us into new dimensions,
holy man dance,
whirling dervish.
Hypnotic
like bicycle wheels,
like church in service.

DIVINE LIGHT

The social contract is broken.

Kimberly Jones

When those in ivory towers,
safe from the threat of a system
that sees them as zeros,
cast judgement faster than tornadoes
spin rooftops in the air,

burrowed deep in the bellies
of Black boys everywhere,
infernos ignite, crackle and Grenfell,
like wildfires devouring captured land.

When they regurgitate news
of an unarmed man slain
by police pistol,
life force drained like muggy water
in the bottom of a bath,
and they don't flinch
because the images the news has quickly gathered
confirm their suspicions (he probably deserved it),

Black boys with their internal organs in flames
breathe fire like purgatory.

It is for our own good;
we just don't know it.

For they are the lighter fluid that keeps the Earth turning,
the redemption that keeps God
from starting all over again.

They see with such clarity;
their ends are nothing
but a surplus of greys and off-browns,
hutches for houses

tucked in the parts of the city
no one wants to see.
These hot-bellied Black boys
are the lights
and the colours
and the comfort, them and their kin.
Without them the borough is all weeds and no trees.

So when these Black boys breathe fire
from the tops of their voices
like town criers in each corner of the city,

I say
let them,
let them
rise from the shattered glass of the shop windows,
laid bare on the floor glistening
as the sun prisms through them.

When those in ivory towers,
safe from the threat of a system
that sees them as zeros,
ask about broken glass
but not broken families,
because they think we have a propensity to be lifeless at the
blast barrel end of a gun,
I see you, my raging lantern brothers.
I promise you,
I get it.

INTUITION

The mothers of the Black children of Bristol
gather and decide the air is not right.

One gets a bloodshot eye.
One cuts her finger while cooking,
while another's mouth tastes like a
flood of copper resin all day.

So when later the children of the city ask
to go to the fair, all of the mothers say no.

Instead the children stay at home;
some go to sleep early,
some play basketball with their friends,
some sit and sulk.

Marlon goes and visit his cousin;
they chat all night long;
the stars fall, the night follows.

Not a crowbar in sight,
no wrenches
nor bats redden by blood,
no knuckle-dented skin;
there is no one screaming ni**r,
no need for CPR or justice campaigns.

DEAD YARD

We give our dead
To the orchards
And the groves.
We give our dead
To life.

Octavia Butler, Parable of the Sower

Where there is death,
there are people gathered for nine nights.
'When the Roll Is Called up Yonder'
is sung by the sisters and brethren in the front room.
Younger cousins sit on the stairs
awaiting the perfect distraction;
when the timing is right
they will swam the kitchen
and procure as many chicken legs
and cans of Fanta as their
dressing-gown pockets can carry.

The women of the family are upstairs,
trying to coax a wailing widow out of bed.
Elsewhere, a man shouts *ludo*
as he slams down his hand,
pieces jump up from the board
and the other men around him groan.

The back door is open;
people are laughing, drinking and recalling stories
of when they were young,
Wata life ina Hngland.
A man cracks open a bottle of white rum
and pours some out for those who have gone.
In the kitchen, a woman scales fish,
other women run about with trays of food,
mutton and rice is everywhere.
Everyone will have a plastic plate soon.

In the back bedroom, older cousins play music and spill tea;
they have a new cousin who is thirteen,
and they are sure he is not the last.
The younger cousins cannot come in.

Funny it is called a dead yard
even when there is so much life.

GRIP

Give good tidings to the strangers,
those who folded their lives
into handheld cases,
flipped it open to recreate home.

If this is wizardry,
the grip must be their magic hat.
Abracadabra,
we are still here.
England is a thing we've survived.

UNFINISHED SYMPATHY: THROWBACK SUITE 2

Girls like me have become accustomed to being asked
where are you from,
where do you belong?
Where is home?
I'm seeking a place for this displaced soul to call home.
In sufi village called Medina Baye
lies my heart, but where is home?
If I'm to believe my birth certificate,
I would say it's Bristol.
But I've been quizzed for so long
and so many times
I'm starting to doubt it.

I was born in Bristol in the eighties.
Posters of rasta babies,
African medallions
and pirate radio stations raised me.
The grey mist of riots never left the air;
blue strobing police sirens left me scared.
I would close my eyes and tense my body, statue-like,
until the gush of wind passed by me
and the wail from the sirens
which in my mind equalled violence
drifted by me like [blow].

I learnt from an early age
you didn't have to commit a crime
when your skin tone stands out like mine;
just being in the wrong place at the wrong time
could mean you had the right face for that crime.
One of the ways that my community lived under
constant scrutiny.
I was born in Bristol in the eighties,
BS2 to be exact.

I heard my city speak in so many different ways,
so many things she tried to articulate under the cover of
shade.
One of the things she could clearly say was music.
Jamaican sound systems to acid jazz,
Pentecostal choirs to Roni Size,
Tricky, Portishead and Massive Attack:
my city had it all.

Bristol was rose reds, royal blues.
She was Black FM discos and frontline videos,
Inkworks and Malcolm X,
the older who remember the bamboo club,
Saturday mornings under hairdryers in Pamsita's
waiting for hot combs to straighten the coils out of my hair.
She was Ivanhoe Campbell pumping Cutty Ranks on the radio,
eclipsed,
grown before her time,
force ripe and shapely,
naive and over-friendly,
ready to extend her hand to anyone who would take it.
Alice lost in a wonderland,
she hid her flaws.
Bristol was beautiful,
but she was also in the midst of a drug epidemic,
a sex epidemic, a keep poor folk poor while
legislators take more epidemic.
I was blind to the pain releasing through her pores;
the power of music had a louder call,
diverted us from all that was wrong and
pointed to something more joyous.
A city covered with dark corners and contradictions
found a beautiful means to cope.

As long as we never dared venture in the parts of town
where your skin could not be brown
because of the legacy of skinheads chasing you down.
So we stayed in our corner

under our stone and made a home
in places most people would not go.
We took pride in our cramped,
our dark, our damp,
in our damnation.
They damned us on TV, in newspapers.
Bushes are overgrown now,
needles on the floor,
elders getting mugged.
Maybe you should leave now,
and some of us did,
left what was once home,
but Black, brown folk are accustomed to doing so.
As we left others came in,
house prices started rising, rent started rising,
so those of us that wanted to stay could not afford to
anyway.
Then they discovered our dark was not so dim;
we are festivals and family gatherings,
entrepreneurs and business owners,
the ones who wake up at
4am to go to work
before we go to our actual work in the morning,
problem solvers,
genius in our dialect,
genius in our intellect,
creators of culture,
rarely beneficiaries of that same culture.
When did we become so profitable?
How do you think Bristol got so mythic?
Legends were here, don't you know?
And you are reaping from the seeds that we sowed.
Bristol was magical.
Unicorns had nothing on us,
and we are still here,
blooming in the underbelly of your mind.

THE CITY

Knelt at your maqam.
Sought your love to no avail.
You sought me right back.
What you seek is seeking you.
Bint Cisse, you loved me first.

BLACK PEOPLE ON TV AGAIN

The era of shouting to siblings and calling friends:
Black people on TV again.
The next day we gather in playgrounds
like water in search of its source,
us morning dew, fresh-faced and fragrant
with youth.
Excitement floods the red brick pathway.
Our chatter cascades over uniformed bodies,
blazers and ties, descends onto assembly lines.
Did you see it?
he says to the girl with the large gold hoop earrings and
the kiwi Body Shop lip balm tightly clutched in her hands,
knowing full well she did,
because that's what young Black girls do
when no one on TV looks like you:
they scan through screens like it is CCTV
in search of a face who too may have got their ears cuffed
with a comb on a Saturday afternoon,
Blue Magic in hand while their mother criss-crossed
tufts of hair into neatly laid crowns.

Someone who too may have a grandma who speaks
a different language or speaks the Queen's English
with a different accent and uses words like
impertinent, contrivance, and says things like
yuh mus use yah discretion.
Yeah, I saw it, it was jokes, she says.
It could have been *Desmond's, Fresh Prince*
or *June Sarpong*
way before conversations of representation.
So when our wavy
stuck-down baby tresses
box braid heroine
Brandy
got her own show
I was glued to every single episode:

Moesha with her band of friends, Hakeem, Niecy,
and of course there was Kim.
For the first time I saw a girl who looked like me,
my age, same size and skin.
The only but was Kim was the butt of every joke:
can't get a man Kim,
inarticulate Kim,
you need to lose weight Kim,
you're not lovable Kim.
Did you hear the one about the big Black girl
who fancied the boy who ran away at every chance
or the one about the big Black girl
who wanted to be a cheerleader
but was too fat to dance?

It took reruns for us to realise our flaws,
poking fun at ourselves, reinventing the caricature
colonisation lent us.
Apparently even the deepest wounds eventually
form a protective crust.
If you don't pick at the scab,
rub lightly, it will eventually fade.
As we begin to repopulate the screens
I wonder if we will poke holes in us again.

WHAT USE ARE WOMEN?

At fifty Janet Jackson birthed a baby boy.
This excites me,
    because how many more periods do I have
      until there is no point
and my period   ends?

This poem doesn't want to come out,
    engage with the fact you may never be born,
    you may be myth and I may be mad,
a cautionary tale for single women not to hope.
Always looking for signs there's still time,
curse myself when I see them,
    reprimand myself when I get excited
    days before a full moon
    when I feel cramps,
the kind that have me rolling on the floor,
clenched like fist,
    cold sweats, vomiting
    over a porcelain bowl,
hoping this means time is on my side.
I've rebuked myself like an old Jamaican woman
    performing an exorcism on the body of her daughter
    who is filled with sin.
Virgin brides are not the only ones wanting
to stain white sheets.
Stained as they are,
my blood clots rarely manifest into full cycles.
    Time is no healer;
    my healing has holes.
I am a holy woman whose whole family
genealogy may end with me.

    You are a child with a name, Rahma or Yasin.
    All the people would say miracle baby,
look how long she had to wait.

I dreamt about you since I was a kid,
    moving through the pages of the Littlewoods catalogues,
wondering where we would live.
I heard your voice,
your heavy foot
    stomping on loosened floorboards in the room above,
    you and your cousins always ramping, making me cuss.

Society tells us we are valuable because our womb works.
What type of woman has a home between her legs
    that men don't want to settle in,
        visitors at best?

What use is a woman who sometimes bleeds?
    What use are women who can't grow a home?

WILLOW GREEN SCHOOL

1.
In the navel of the green of the infant school I used to attend
stands a queenly oversized willow tree.
Sophie says, *If only the trees could talk.*

Those trees and their queen have witnessed our everything:
our sapling, our bloom, our withering until next season.

Willow trees have a great chance of thriving
where the air is cold
and the soil is moist,
or at least they remain alive.
If this is the case we have much in common:
England, the perfect place for foreign bodies
to call home.

This is less true with each new government, each new policy.
We are weeping willows.
Some grow just centimetres high,
while few manage to tower above the rest,
sending down their viney leaves in hopes that we will touch.
There is no way to know which ones will do best,
but never do the trees and their queen stop witnessing us.

2.
This is my favourite season,
when the earth is moist
and the air is crisp.

Foliage deviates from its colour before it
surrenders to the ground,
a leafy mosaic:

sinopia, akhdar, brick red and brass
reflecting the sun and bouncing off everything in sight.

The middle of the school playground is where I scale,
witnessing everybody's everythings.
I love it like the day kiss chases the night
and Muslims love to fast.

Even in the damp of the season, I'm fragrant
like musk, oud and natural browns.
Maybe that's why people flock
to me like I am Jesus Christ,

come to me like children to cake-mixed spoons,
take comfort in my solid body, seek salvation in
the braille of my branches
as if my weeping can wail away their woes.

SCREAM

Scream: Verb
/skri:m/
screamed; screaming; screams

Entry 1
Emotions manifested on earth through sound.
Keeps composure,
absorbs negativity that floats in the air like lint.
Some wear it across their faces before they swim into a sea of
puffed-up pillow
I've worn it too.

The one I remember the most
was when I knew it was the end of us.
I had sucked in my belly,
held my mouth,
swallowed my voice.
My body was swollen with words that made me shrink.
Even my shadow knew not to hang around.
I used to feel ashamed by the things I made normal.
I think that's how it's supposed to work.
You get away with it because I am silent.

Entry 2
That scream was blissful,
cathartic.
Even you looked scared,
like I would shred you to papier-mâché,
spit you out like chewed-up trash of sugarcane,
you stale chewing gum with grit from the pavement
on the bottom of my beat-up Vans.
That was my trophy
my gnaw-your-ear off moment,
my mouth all bloody.

Your earlobe throbbing on the floor,
flipping about like a goldfish out of water.
Call me sadistic,
but the taste of blood still excites me
and to this day gives me life.

PROPHECY

There are those who brandish badges,
carry batons
and now guns.
They are coming for yours too.
You won't be able to seek solace in songs like
at least we are not America.
It will not just be our siblings and children
piling up at the chapel of rest.
Then you will know what we have always known:
there are many ways to skin a cat.

NEW

PRAYER

Crack of dawn, **break** of night.
Our body knows how to **contour** us into **submission**.
We twist and turn, then bend in sujood and ruku.
How many times have we had to spring new limbs,
start again?
Felt hurt and caught shivers from the pain?
We are stars glimmering, so when we are down,
it is here that we go for light.

AL-QAABID

Surely after hardship there is ease, most certainly after hardship there is ease
Quran Surah 94:6–7

The night is buried in an endless hole that is a womb.
Cascading into darkness is nothing but embryonic fluids
and life; this is birth,
nothing but umbilical cord tight around your neck,
gripping as you wheeze in search of air,
nothing but contractions,
dilation, birth and growth.
The dark holds us,
wrenched us like daffodils plucked in springtime
into existence out of nothing,
kun faya kun.
The perfect backdrop for us to glow
catches us as we descend into
collapsing gases and burnt-out suns.
They got it right,
those who wander in congregations,
attired in lightless hoodies,
and live in it like it's skin.
These glowing Black sons know
light is its brightest against a backdrop of black;
not all that is bright is warm.
Thank God for the
silhouettes and shadows
that highlight our shades and contours.

OUD

From the rib   of the tree

via the root,   this liquid

flowers the   wearer

like she is   fruit.

DEAR BODY: THROWBACK SUITE 3

Dear body,
thick body,
brown body,
round, curved, clutch body,
soft body,
my body soaked in lavender
with a fragrance somewhere between mangos and vanilla
body,
dear you.
Stout like your grandma,
curved like your mama,
thick-skinned and supple heart,
blemished skin and breaking heart.
Sorry for the times I've neglected you,
failed to shower you with gratitude.
You are more than vessel,
more like vital,
without you this world void and without form,
no thought, feeling, nor functioning,
no witnessing God wanting to be known,
no stumbling over SubhanAllah
when hearing it the very first time,
no bended knees, nor fajr tears,
no closed eyes when kissed on the neck,
nor faint breath when kissed on my back.
Dear body,
my carry me through hurt body,
compartmentalised until I could deal with body,
heal with body,
I have neglected you,
bitched at you,
bullied you for being so:
so fat,
so dark,
so light,
so hair not long enough,
hair too thick under my chin,

breasts too big,
butt too small,
feet too flat,
shoulders too broad.
How have you coped,
not broken down, body?
Even when you were pinned down
and screamed out,
and once again you were pinned down
but learnt not to scream out,
'cause last time there was nobody,
just you and somebody
who wished to colonise you
like a country rich in resources,
mother tongue gone;
all that remains is corrupted languages
that have taught us not to love our bodies,
so it's no wonder I've neglected you,
at one point even loathed you.
But now
I need you to know you are heavenly,
the type of body that continents
could be named after:
Muuuuuu Neeer Rah.
Land of silk tongues and wild ravines,
stretch marks carved in tummies and thighs,
land bountiful and overflowing.
House of hope,
home of hearts,
you are loved,
thick body,
brown body,
round, curved, clutch body,
soft body.
Thank you for carrying me through.

ODE TO MY FACIAL HAIR

For the hours spent as a child on the side of my bath
staring at my mother, learning the art of womanhood.

The pounds and time spent chasing away shadows above
my lip, chin, neck, and the side of my face.

For the burns and sores left behind by Veet,
which could not coax into submission the thick hair from my
face.

For the friend I lost, his aunt who was more like his mother;
young, dumb me mocked her for having stubble like mine.

For the peach fluff, the creams, the wax, the strips,
the thread for threading, blades for dermablading,

the cotton balls for the spots of blood,
tweezers for the ingrown hairs when they need a tug.

For the shadows that stalk my face, my face that looks like
my mother, like my grandmother, and probably her mother
too.

Here's to my skin, the body I'm in
and the hair that sprouts like roots.

MELAHFA/TOOB

Girls who ride the number 18 bus and the 266,
who are vegan some months
but can murder a mixed lamb and chicken shawarma
from Maroush on others,
who love Reebok Classics,
gassing with their besties
about their latest situationships.
Girls who wear red lipstick,
listen to Kaytranada,
Ghetts and Wu-Tang,
who consider muttah – *I swear down* –
and have a thing for dark-skinned dudes
with thick beards;
too
dream
of losing themselves in deserts
where they wrap themselves in melahfas and toobs,
look like
Hagar,
Rabia al-Adawiyya,
and think about nothing but God,
Black henna-painted fingertips
flicking the balls from their dhikr beads
as if on the other side heaven awaits,
cover their faces,
lower their gaze,
sit at the feet of their shaykh
and sing songs of praise.

MUNIR

Us
marigold, geometry and light
poured into vessel,
astronomy, histories and stories
spilling out like pillow talk
from the mouth of a lover
delicately moulded into motion.
Blissful dreams
only a creator could conjure,
lasting prayer from our ancestors
suspended in time.
There are pieces of
us
puzzled around the planet;
placed in our chest
is the desire to gather them.
What a sweet equation,
the answer to all the things not yet solved.
If God is a beauty that wants to be known,
then we are seekers and seamen,
nomads and pilgrims,
sojourners and travellers in search of God's light,
Sallahu Alayhi wa Salam.

LIKE MALCOLM

You used to
collect stamps,
comics,
coins,
rare toy cars,
collect Action Man figures
you were into art.
Some had a collection of broken hearts;
not young you.
You were into collecting
Nintendo games,
forehead kisses from your aunty,
food in Tupperware from your grandma
that she knew you would never return.
You even collected bad wad if you stepped out of line.

On the other side of town
you collected a body of stab wounds
confettied around your lungs.
Gurgles and bubbles collected to form a strawberry-stained mouth.
They collected you in an ambulance.
Alhamdulillah you survived.

You never stopped collecting, though!
Stitches,
multiple operations,
seedless grapes and bottles of original flavour Lucozade;
you collected anger,
pain,
breathing problems.
You collected fear,
and then something in you changed.

Your collection grew more extravagant, a connoisseur of sorts.
You collected clothes,
cars,

collected girls and side pieces
that would hold onto your side pieces,
collected more stab wounds,
more near misses,
dashes down the stairs of South London estates,
collected lucky escapes
and a set of new friends,
collected bags of brown and white powder
and started selling them,
laughs,
bravado,
ego,
until one collection went wrong.
Now you collect call and reverse the charges,
collect your thoughts,
collect memories of before.
Your angels collect notes
of the thousands of Yasins you've recited.
Collect Quran verses and istagfirAllahs.
Collect yourself like Malcolm and pray salah.

WHEN THEY SPEAK OF MUSLIMS

They are not speaking of wallahi,
Nike Air Huaraches,
five wings and chips, boss,
false lashes,
turbans and black hijabs,
gold teeth, Jordans, jelbabs and black niqabs.

They are not speaking of halal beef patties,
Salatul Fatih,
Ayatul Kursi,
uhktis and ahkis.

They are not speaking of Fatima who is also Tracey,
nor Mohammed who is sometimes Mo.

They are not speaking of jazz, blues and bebop,
Pharoah Sanders or A Love Supreme,
reggae sound systems
and the soundmen who have found Allah,
of Marcus Garvey and Bob Marley,
Krept, Konan or Little Simz.

They are not speaking of people the colour of ravens,
nor diamond-chiselled cheeks constructed on the jaw.

They are not speaking of rubies where the whites should be,
nor black pupils that eclipse and cling like darts.

They do not speak of crocky high-pitched women
somewhere between crooning and beseeching,
singing and forecasting,
Sallahu Alayhi wa Salam
after each phrase,
perched on rusted stools,
old Coke crates
or tattered old red and green mats made of plastic wicker.

In England they are decorative;
elsewhere they are for prayer and dhikr.

Not speaking of forty bodies stowed in the back of a lorry,
chartered flights to a place that is no longer home.

They are not speaking of crumpled papers
that state you have the right to remain,
the ones police have the right to restrain,
right to prevent oxygen from getting to the brain.

Instead they are speaking of Rumi,
of wise men,
of Orion.
They liked me better back then.

DHIKR BEADS

Each flick draws you in.
You didn't know you were thirsting,
but the utterance of God's name
muttered under your breath
is soothing,
the repetition lulls your body.
Eyes closed,
you rock like waves.

This rendezvous pulls you in,
uncloaks you,
substitutes you for it.
You'll call God's names
and forget you used to exist.

THE TOBAB BLACK GIRLS OF MEDINA BAYE

Inspired by 'The Puerto Rican Girls of French Hill' by Sean Thomas Dougherty.

The Tobab Black girls
of Medina Baye
glisten like
Sadina Muhammed durrasoolullah
Sallahu Alayhi wa Salam
like noor
dripping
from dhikr beads
residue
on their face
glow like
brown wet henna
before it dries
Senegalese gold
and Tuareg silver
aqeeq rings
on the hands
of the Awaliy
inheritors
of God
they supplicate
a dua
so sincere
in English
broken/Arabic
and barely Wolof
hat tricks
couldn't
shoot nor score
more succinctly
than their lips
that pray at night

and say *la illah illallah*
in masjids with
green domes and maqams
in blessed villages
where love
of
Allah
is rife

HIS NAME

Ya Noor
Ya Saraj
Ya Misbah
Rasul Al Rahma
Nabiyy Al Fatah
The mention of your name is a baraka.
Your name in our hearts is a baraka.
Seed bloom into trees,
trees bear fruits and leaves and we are left in the spring of you,
Sadina Muhammed Sallahu Alayhi wa Salam.

TO ALL THE MEN WHO USE 'WHY ARE YOU SINGLE' AS A CHAT-UP LINE

They ask me why I'm single.
I shy away from the truth.
Spiritual women attract broken men,
and like a nurse I tend to them.
It's not that I've never had relationships.
It's just there's a thin line between lover and healer;
I am often both and he is often neither.

He is the one in need,
and I mostly have the ability
to rejuvenate when I deplete.

They come to me wounded,
and it would seem my womb
has a thing for making my heart their remedy.
Them idling on sacred ground,
somebody else's sacred house.
I act placid as they set God's house alight to keep them warm.
When they're done I put out their flames with acid,
scooping up the flesh that's left behind,
knowing these scars will heal with time.
Because who does not want a woman
who can heal like alchemy,
who can ease pain and sorrow,
mixing elixirs out of her tears, cloves and aloes?
Who does not want a woman who will give all of herself
until she is hollow, God's home is hollow?
I am shallow, yet drowning still.
It's best I'm single; that's God's will.
Pen has lifted feather and quill.
We are remodelling,
house into a home,
so the next man who enters
will have to take off his shoes and bow to God's throne.

NOTES ON THE POEMS

Opening: In Islam the first chapter of the Quran is called Al Fatiha, which translates as 'opening'. As this poem is the first poem of the book, I wanted to in some way acknowledge that through the grace of God, by way of my mother, I have been given an opening to write my very first collection.

Sweetback: This poem references a time when I worked for the Sony Street Team and I used to get prereleases of records. The record in question is 'You Will Rise' by Sweetback, which featured Amel Larrieux from the group Groove Theory.

Blue Magic: Blue Magic is a hair pomade that many young Black girls, certainly in the western hemisphere, used in order to keep their hair and scalp moisturised in the ritual process of plaiting hair.

Black Cherry Lipstick: Black Cherry is a shade of lipstick that seemed to be worn exclusively by Black girls in Bristol in the late nineties. Very few shops stocked it, and it would be often placed in the most undesirable part of the shop.

Skin a Cat: Inspired by the book *Between the World and Me* by Ta-Nehisi Coates and an episode of *Another Round* podcast with hosts Tracy Clayton and Heben Nigatu, featuring Bim Adewunmi.

Cousins: This poem was inspired by a poem of the same name by Kevin Young, found in his collection *Dear Darkness.*

Ragga FM: This poem is inspired by the UK pirate radio station movement, particularly the pirate radio stations in Bristol that shaped me, raised me and sometimes broke my heart.

Divine Light: Inspired by the Gal Dem, Man Dem, People Dem, Elders Dem, whose bellies fill with a righteous fire and a desire for justice in the face of wrongdoing and apathy. Inspired by the prayers that keep us safe and bring us closer to healing.

Intuition: Inspired by the poem 'For Trayvon Martin' by Reuben Jackson and a poem by Rakaya Fetuga called 'For Grenfell'. The poem makes reference to the violent attack on Marlon Thomas at Bristol Durham Downs by Bob Wilson Fair workers in March 1993. May we never forget.

The City: Inspired by my shaykh, Shaykh Mahy Cisse, and the blessed city of Medina Baye.

Black People on TV Again: Inspired by the greatness of Black sitcoms of the late nineties and early 2000s.

Munir: Inspired by one of the names of the Prophet Muhammed peace be upon him, Munir, which roughly translate as 'guiding light'.

The Tobab Black Girls of Medina Baye: Inspired by 'The Puerto Rican Girls of French Hill' by Sean Thomas Dougherty, and by the Black girls who travel across the world to seek God.

Red Lipstick, Blue Magic and **Melahfa/Toob** were filmed as part of the Greenbelt film commission No Normal in 2021. You can watch by scanning the QR code below:

Lessons Taught to Boys and Girls was filmed as part of the Bristol Old Vic Sudden Connections commission in 2021.

Unfinished Sympathy was commissioned and appeared as part of TEDx Bristol in 2019. You can watch by scanning the QR code below:

Munir was commissioned by Manifesting the Unseen for their exhibition of the same name in 2021.

Al-Qaabid was commissioned by Raise Karma in 2021.

To All the Men Who Use 'Why Are You Single' as a Chat-Up Line appeared on Radio 4's *Beyond Belief*, recorded live at the Contains Strong Language poetry Festival in 2021.

GRATITUDES

Alhamdulillah! I finally get to write the gratitudes for my debut collection, and I know it reads like an acceptance speech, but 'llow me, please!

SubhanAllah there is so much to be grateful for, and I know in the excitement I am going to miss something or someone, so first thing, I seek forgiveness for anything wrong between these pages, and praise Allah for any good that you see.

There have been so many people instrumental in putting together this collection, the first being Shagufta K Iqbal, who ignited in me the possibility.

Abdul-Rehman Malik, who told me a book was the natural next step and who continues to advocate for me in rooms where I am absent: the amount of opportunity that has come my way by virtue of the seeds that you've sown is ridiculous. My dear little sis and teacher Rakaya Fetuga, thank you for going on those makeshift writing retreats with me, being a listening ear, and answering my calls when I would ask, 'Which word sounds better?'

Dear Jacob Sam-La Rose, great writer, poet, teacher, human being, and cultivator of meaningful connection. What you have done for me is more than I can express. What I can say is that I am forever changed as a poet, and I will continue to strive as a poet and human as a result of our conversations.

Suhaiymah Manzoor-Khan, you may not know it, but working with you on other projects while in the process of writing this book was precious. You comforted me when I was scared my book was not as political or spiritual as my previous work; you allowed me to see that all my stories are political, all my stories are spiritual, all my stories are valuable and worthy of being heard.

Dear Sarina Mantle or Mama Wild Suga, thank you for gracing me with your exquisite artwork and the conversation around the need to have Black faces, my face on the cover of my book; it feels like an act of resistance, so thank you, my sister comrade!

Thank you, David Mensah, for your wonderful photos of me and putting up with my impromptu poetry listening parties where you are the only audience member.

Thank you to Hafsa Hassan and Nora Musa for celebrating the poetry collection and celebrating me, and pushing me to shout about my work.

Thank you to the Poetry Society for being on the other end of the phone whenever I had questions.

To the homie, Dom G! You have listened to me all throughout this process, cleared emails when I didn't have the energy, given me level-headed advice and so much more. I appreciate you.

To my dear Simone Talbert, Shaheen Kasmani, Sophia Mighty, Hudda Khaireh and Ebony Kerr, thank you for being my sounding board, and my loves.

My publisher, Burning Eye: thank you, you wonderful people!

Bridget, you have calmed me in panic attacks, comforted me when I'm anxious and depressed, you give me your food when I order the wrong food, and you have not cancelled me or the publication even when I've avoided you. Harriet, I've always known I love people who push me to be better, and even though I have never met you, is it strange to say I think I love you? This book would be nothing without your technical edits and comments in the margins.

Dear Clive, again for conversations about my face on the cover and your general support, thank you!

BE crew, thank you.

There is no Muneera Pilgrim without the journey of Poetic Pilgrimage, and no PP without Sukina Pilgrim. Ups and downs, good and bad, hotel rooms, eviction notices, flights, bus stops, bust-ups, conversions to Islam, embracing a tariqa. Know there is always love.

To the Fetuga family, thank you for your nurturing and love. My Zone Ones, my Day Ones, my Black Girl Con family, Project Zazi family, my Tijani family, my Muslim family worldwide.

Thank you to the UK Black cycling community. I appreciate a place where thriving and joy is the focus.

To Tanya and Sike, the best housemates a girl could ask for.

To Shaykh Michael Mumisa, you have been invaluable to my journey.

My brothers Rakin and Ismael, thank you for the guidance from day dot.

To the late Faud Nahdi, thank you for your vision and belief.

To the friend I am no longer in a friendship with, I mourn your loss, but hold on to how your love helped me to grow.

To my collective ::NANA::, SariayaBah.

To my poetry peers and friends, the hip-hop community that embraced PP, much love.

To all of the organisations and individuals who championed me or paid me well, ETT and IBT for my first residentials, Everyday Muslim project for your trust in the face of my longness. Thank you all!

To the creative Black Muslim community, particularly those in the UK, I see you, shining, and I am honoured to be of you. Thank you.

To my beautiful parents who have facilitated and supported me in so many ways, ways that I did not recognise at times. Forgive me for my ignorance and thank you for your love. I thank God for your everything!

My siblings, y'all wild at times, but I would be deficient without you.

My nieces and nephews, you give me life, I love you to no end.

To all of my family, you know what it is, I love you.

To those in my life who have not made me feel guilty or stupid throughout my struggles with depression and anxiety, I promise you it is a rare love language.

To you the reader, thank you for witnessing me and connecting with me in this way.

To Shaykh Mahy Cisse, I know your prayers sustain me; thank you beyond words. May Allah bless you, all of your works, and all of your family. May Allah allow me to be of your spiritual lineage, and allow me to be faithful and true.

In the name of Allah the Most Gracious the Most Merciful, by the Blessing of the Prophet Muhammed Sallahu Alahiy wa Salam I am so blessed and so thankful, Alhamdulillah.

If you ever felt marginalised, or not centred, know your story is important, sing your song loud.
In the words of Solange Knowles: this one's for us!

May we be blessed.

Muneera <3

Sign up to Muneera's mailing list here:

Lightning Source UK Ltd.
Milton Keynes UK
UKHW011917220222
399081UK00001B/49